First Visit to the Dentist with Abby

Whitney Sanderson

Lerner Publications ◆ Minneapolis

Discover six early milestones alongside your favorite *Sesame Street* friends! From visiting the dentist to getting a library card, this series helps young children feel prepared for new and exciting experiences that are a part of growing up.

Sincerely,
The Editors at Sesame Workshop

Table of Contents

Healthy Teeth, Healthy You

A dentist is a doctor for your teeth. They help you keep your teeth clean and healthy.

I'm excited to visit the dentist!

When you visit the dentist, they will check your teeth.

If there is a problem, they help fix it!

Going to the Dentist

Many dentists have helpers called hygienists. A hygienist will call you from the waiting room and bring you to a big chair where you'll get your teeth checked and cleaned.

The big chair at my dentist's office goes up and down and tilts back too.

The dentist or the hygienist will use a tool called an explorer to count your teeth and check that they are healthy.

I love when the dentist counts my teeth! Ah, ah, ah!

They will use a tool called a polisher to get your teeth extra clean. It is a special kind of toothbrush.

The polisher tickles!

The toothpaste they use comes in different flavors, like mint or strawberry. Sometimes you can pick the flavor you want!

They'll also use dental floss to clean the spaces between your teeth.

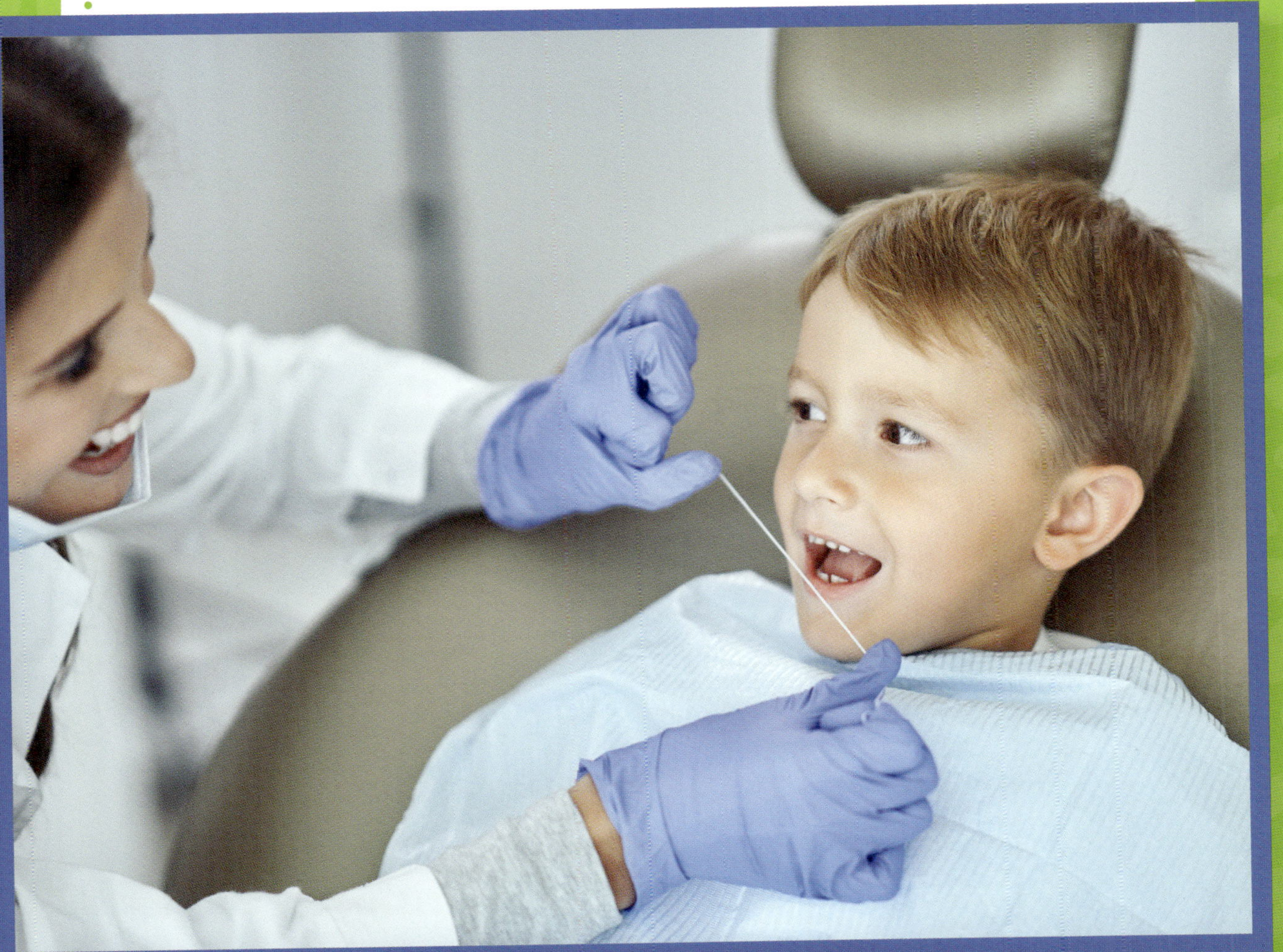

Sometimes they take X-rays, or pictures of your teeth. You might wear a big, heavy apron during the X-rays. Stay as still as you can so the picture is clear.

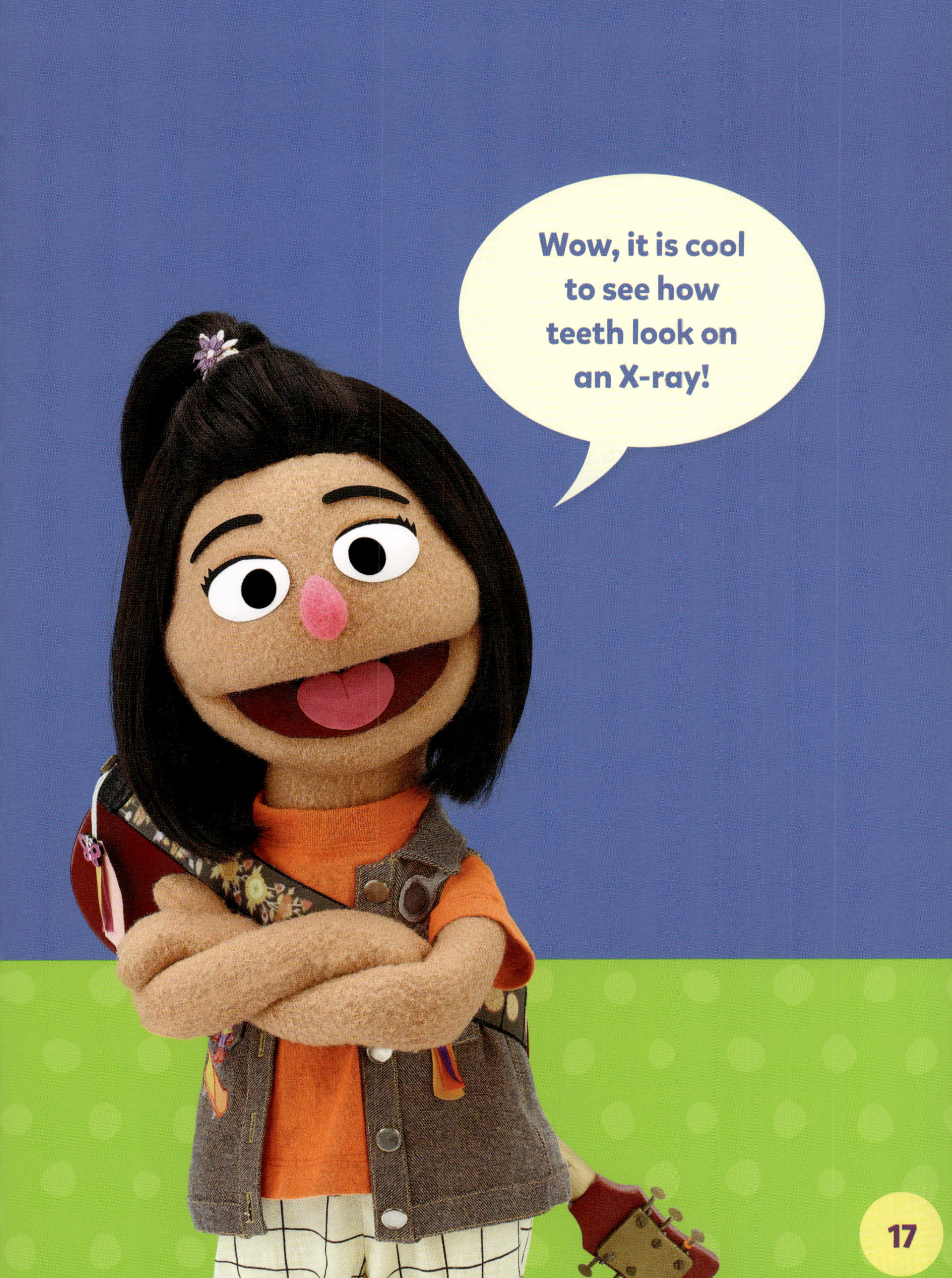
Wow, it is cool to see how teeth look on an X-ray!

Once your teeth are clean, the dentist or the hygienist might put fluoride on your teeth. It helps your teeth stay strong.

Strong teeth
mean healthy
teeth!

The dentist will tell you how to take care of your teeth. This will help keep your teeth clean and healthy between checkups!

Get Ready for Your Dentist Visit

It's important to brush your teeth twice a day. When you brush, do the following:

1. Wet your toothbrush with water.
2. Put a small amount of toothpaste on your brush.
3. Brush in tiny, gentle circles. Make sure to brush the front, back, top, and bottom.
4. Brush for two minutes.
5. Spit out the toothpaste. Rinse your mouth and your toothbrush with water. Great job!

Glossary

dental floss: thin string you pull back and forth between your teeth to clean them

dentist: a person who helps take care of your teeth

fluoride: a liquid or foam that dentists apply to help keep your teeth strong

hygienist: a person who helps a dentist care for your teeth

Read More

Cipriano, Jeri. *Going to the Dentist.* Egremont, MA: Red Chair, 2022.

Gabor, Nicole. *First Lost Tooth with Gabrielle.* Minneapolis: Lerner Publications, 2026.

Murray, Julie. *A Visit to the Dentist.* Minneapolis: Abdo Kids, 2024.

Photo Acknowledgments

Image credits: Peter Dazeley/Getty Images, p. 3; Zinkevych/Getty Images, p. 4; Jacob Wackerhausen/Getty Images, p. 6; shironosov/Getty Images, p. 8; monkeybusinessimages/Getty Images, p. 10; Rabizo Anatolii/Shutterstock, p. 12; macniak/Getty Images, p. 15; Javier Zayas Photography/Getty Images, p. 16; Kobus Louw/Getty Images, p. 18; yamasan/Getty Images, p. 21. Design element: Agunar/Shutterstock.

Cover: undefined undefined/Getty Images.

Index

To Faisal

Lerner Publications Company
An imprint of Lerner Publishing Group, Inc.
241 First Avenue North
Minneapolis, MN 55401 USA

For reading levels and more information, look up this title at www.lernerbooks.com.

Main body text set in MIkado.
Typeface provided by HvD Fonts.

Library of Congress Cataloging-in-Publication Data

Names: Sanderson, Whitney, author.
Title: First visit to the dentist with Abby / Whitney Sanderson.
Description: Minneapolis : Lerner Publications, [2026] | Series: Sesame street firsts | Includes bibliographical references and index. | Audience: Ages 4–8 | Audience: Grades K–1 | Summary: "Dentists help people take care of their teeth and stay healthy. Young readers learn along with their Sesame Street friends what to expect at their first visit to the dentist"— Provided by publisher.
Identifiers: LCCN 2024037454 (print) | LCCN 2024037455 (ebook) | ISBN 9798765661031 (lib. bdg.) | ISBN 9798765684818 (pbk.) | ISBN 9798765680858 (epub)
Subjects: LCSH: Children—Preparation for dental care—Juvenile literature. | Dentists—Juvenile literature. | Teeth—Care and hygiene—Juvenile literature.
Classification: LCC RK63 .S26 2026 (print) | LCC RK63 (ebook) | DDC 617.6/45—dc23/eng/20241210

LC record available at https://lccn.loc.gov/2024037454
LC ebook record available at https://lccn.loc.gov/2024037455

Manufactured in the United States of America
1-1011808-53658-12/9/2024